A YAK'S CORNER BOOK

Detroit Free Press

CREDITS

Stories brought to you by Yak's Corner staffers
Patricia Chargot, Janis Campbell and Catherine Wilde Collison.

Also contributing were Marcy Abramson, David Crumm and
Heather Newman of the Detroit Free Press.

Art director and book design: Marty Westman.

Cover photography and styling: J. Kyle Keener.
Cover design: Marty Westman.

Book editors: Catherine Wilde Collison, Janis Campbell and Marcy
Abramson.

Photo technicians: Christine Russell and Jessica Trevino.
Additional photos and graphics from Detroit Free Press archives.

Additional thanks to students at Roeper School,
Birmingham/Bloomfield Hills, Michigan.

For more stories and adventures from the Yak, visit our Web site at
www.yakscorner.com

For information about our syndicated section for young readers, write:
Editor, Yak's Corner
P.O. Box 170
Detroit, MI 48231

ISBN 0-937247-30-8

CONTENTS

WELCOME TO THE YAKLENNIUM

YAKTIVITIES:

You'll see this symbol throughout the book. It's our Yaktivity symbol, a sign that there's something to do!

WELCOME to the Yaklennium

What's that? It's what we're calling the new millennium — the next 1,000 years.

We named it after the Yak, the mascot of the national newspaper for kids, created at the Detroit Free Press.

Here at Yak's Corner, we are curious and just a little scared. Thinking about what the next 1,000 years could be like is enough to boggle a Yak's mind. So we asked our Yak's Corner staff to check out the upcoming century — especially the next couple of years. What did they find?

There are problems — some big ones. But the folks we yakked with also pointed to solutions. And the solutions probably won't come from adults; they'll come from kids like you who are in elementary and middle school now. The classes of 2004 to 2010 — that's who will be leading the way into the millennium.

We talked to Yak's Corner panelists too, to get their wish lists. You'll meet them in this section. Maybe all their goals won't be met, at least right now, but they sure got us thinking. What stood out was how closely linked we will be in the new millennium. Lives around the world will be more interwoven than ever before — through technology, through the environment and through classrooms.

Hmmm ... what would a day be like?

Imagine a world where all the cars are pollution-free and everyone car pools to work or school. Or kids can walk to school, even in winter, because sidewalks are smooth and warm from underground heating. All kids carry a small, extra-light laptop computer in their backpacks. No way you can forget homework — it's on the computer. You play games on computers no bigger than a key chain. You haven't had any sick days from school because your food contains all the vaccines you need to stay healthy.

And just for fun, you can take a weekend trip — a class overnight in outer space.

Possible? Maybe not tomorrow, or not even in the next couple of years. But when you think about the new Yaklennium, the sky — and beyond — is the limit.

TIME FOR AN ADVENTURE

It's about time.

That's what brought the Yak to stand high on a hill above the Thames River in England, under misty skies, with one hoof in the east and another hoof in the west.

He was in Greenwich, England, straddling the line — marked by people — that long ago was chosen as zero degrees longitude, or the Prime Meridian. The Prime Meridian is the line running from the north to the south pole that's used to measure the east and west. But more about that later.

The Yak was curious. Where could he go to find out about time — and sort out the confusion over when the new millennium starts and just how we measure such things?

Some British schoolkids were running down the hill — placing a backpack of toys and stuffed animals along it. They were there for a project for a British television station, trying to illustrate a time line.

They told the Yak to head inside to the Greenwich Royal Observatory. It's always been a great museum, but now is the focus of lots of millennium questers. "The official starting point of the new Millennium," say the signs.

You see, Greenwich is where east meets west. Back in 1675, Sir Christopher Wren built the Royal Observatory in Greenwich. (He designed lots of the famous buildings in London, including St. Paul's Cathedral.) At that time, Greenwich was enough out in the country that it was a great place for astronomers! Greenwich was a busy

Greenwich is the place known as the center of time! That's why the Yak visited.

This contraption is a clock made by John Harrison in the 18th Century. It was a new type of clock — without a pendulum.

port, but not as busy as London. Up on the hill, you could build a great place to watch the stars. King Charles II wanted the observatory to help solve a big problem for his sailors. He was hoping the astronomers could solve the longitude problem and that would lead England's ships to be tops in navigating the seas.

But they had a problem in measuring. Longitude is measuring how far east or west you are. Latitude is how far north and south — and could be measured from the Equator. How did they measure longitude? It's linked to time. Sailors would check on the local time — from positions of sun or stars or moon — and compare them to the time back home. Then they would know how far east or west they had sailed.

We really don't have time for the whole story. But it didn't take us too many minutes to walk through the observatory to see where the astronomers looked for solutions — and to see how people kept inventing better clocks and ways to measure time. We saw sundials and hourglasses.

We learned that measuring time at sea was so important that by 1714, the British government offered a BIG reward to someone to find a way to do it.

Lots of people thought an astronomer would get the prize. But the hero of the story was John Harrison, a carpenter and clockmaker, who invented a new type of clock that didn't need a pendulum. That way it could measure time and not be affected by the motion of a ship.

At the Royal Observatory at Greenwich, a time ball drops from the top of a pole at one o'clock each afternoon. Sailors on the Thames River would use the ball's drop to set their chronometer clocks.

Prize people quibbled and weren't willing to give him the prize at first — but he kept making better clocks. His H4, a seagoing clock or chronometer, would allow people to measure time directly from any town or city.

Still, there was more trouble. People didn't have a uniform measurement. By the 1880s, lots of countries were doing measuring for ships, but each would measure from a different meridian — any north-south line used to measure traveling east and west. With all the shipping traffic growing, people had a big meeting in Washington, D.C., and voted that the meridian line through the eyepiece of the telescope in Greewnich would be the Prime Meridian. That means it's the zero point on the globe and everything's position is measured from that line. This led to our current time zones for the world.

It works this way: When it's midnight on the Greenwich Prime Meridian, that's the start of the day. Every other time zone is calculated based on Greenwich time.

Now let's finish our tour of the museum.

We had walked through the displays of old clocks and new. The weather was clearing and we could go back outside again, on the way checking out the millennium countdown clock.

Time to move on.

By Cathy Collison

Photos courtesy of the Royal Observatory at Greenwich.

Even at night, the Prime Meridian is marked with lights and a line in the walkway at Greenwich.

LOG SOME TIME ON THE WEB

Take a virtual field trip to Greenwich and the Millennium Dome. Head first to **greenwich2000.com** and you'll feel like you're a time traveler. There's plenty of fun stuff on the Millennium Dome and much more about the history of time.

WHEN IS THE TRUE MILLENNIUM?

You can celebrate the year turning 2000, but 2001 is the true start of the millennium.

Here's why, say the scientists at the Royal Greenwich Observatory. (The observatory itself is celebrating with a special millennium party and other projects in 2000 and 2001.)

A millennium is a period of 1,000 years. The calendar the United States generally uses is based on the Christian calendar, which is broken into parts. The Christian calendar dates from BC, before Christ, to AD, which means anno domini — year of the Lord — in Latin.

When the calendar was created, long after Christ's death, it ran like this: 3BC, 2 BC, 1 BC, AD 1, AD 2, AD 3. There was no zero year named. Adding it that way means the year 2000 is the last of this millennium and 2001 starts the new one. The first century began at the start of year one, the second century at the year 101 and the 20th Century began at the start of the year 1901.

(Remember, this calendar isn't shared by everyone. The year 2000, for example, starts in the fourth month of the Jewish year 5760 and the ninth month of the Muslim year 1420.)

Photos courtesy of Millennium Experience

If you are celebrating, when do you do it?

Lots of people will celebrate in 2000, even the scientists. Not far from the observatory in Greenwich, there's a giant Millennium Dome built for the occasion. Because Greenwich is the place where time begins, in a way, it's only right to have a huge place for people to party. It's open to mark the first celebrations in 2000. And it will be open for more events right through the official millennium in 2001. Expect lots of celebrations — whether they're celebrating the 2000th year or the last year of the old millennium in 2000.

There's plenty of time!

By Cathy Collison

The Millennium Dome in Greenwich is the scene of celebration and is built on the Prime Meridian.

TIME FOR ACTIVITY

You can always make time for fun and interesting activities. Here are some timely ideas to try:

HOURGLASS

The hourglass has been used as a way to tell time for ages. The principle is simple: Time is measured by how long the sand takes to run from the top to the bottom. Many cooks still use one- or three-minute timers.

You can do some simple experiments with clear glasses and funnels. Try different amounts of sand. See how fast the sand flows through the funnel. Once you've experimented, you can label the glass and funnel. Now you can have a set of 1-minute, 5-minute and even 10-minute timers in your class or home.

ON YOUR MARK, SET YOUR CLOCKS

If you have extra clocks in the classroom, or at home, make an international wall of clocks. Set four or more clocks to different time zones in the world. Start by making one clock for your town and one clock on Greenwich time.

WHAT'S YOUR LONGITUDE?

It's fun to stand on the Prime Meridian, as the Yak did. Not everyone can get to England, but you can mark out the longitude of your school on the playground or down the hallway. Then research what other places around the world share the same longitude, but different latitude. See if you can find a school with the same longitude in another part of the country — or world. Then exchange e-mail and letters!

RHYME TIME

It's not only sailors and clock makers who are fascinated with time. The passing of time is a timely subject for poets and musicians. You probably know the nursery rhyme, "Hickory dickory dock, the mouse ran up the clock." And have you heard the rock oldie, "Rock Around the Clock"?

Try to write your own time rhyme or time tune. To get you started, here are some words that use time: suppertime, overtime, halftime, time out! Time to go!

SOME BIG PROBLEMS, BUT WE CAN FIX THEM

The 20th Century really changed people's lives. Imagine life without telephones, radio, television or computers! Technology — such as space-based telescopes and the space shuttle — is so advanced that humans now reach into all of the world's environments. But we've created some big problems: global warming, ozone holes, the threatened extinction of many plant and animal species. At least seven countries have nuclear weapons. An accident at a nuclear power plant could release deadly radioactivity, and nuclear waste will remain dangerous for centuries. The good news is that we've never had better tools with which to study our problems and solve them. But scientists say everyone on the planet will have to be involved. Will you be?

IT'S TIME FOR THE EARTH TO CHILL

"I believe we have an obligation to fight for life on Earth — not just for ourselves, but for all those who, if we are wise enough, will come after."

— Carl Sagan

Scientists everywhere are worried about the Earth's future. One was Carl Sagan, the famous astronomer who wrote the novel "Contact," which became a movie starring Jodie Foster.

Sagan, who died in 1996, was really good at explaining complicated problems, such as global warming, to people who aren't scientists. He and others have tried to get the word out, but a lot of people still don't know what's happening.

Probably the biggest problem Earth faces is global warming, or the heating up of the atmosphere due to carbon dioxide — called CO_2 — and other

greenhouse gases.

Until recently, some scientists didn't believe the warming was real. Computer models and information collected near the Earth's surface showed a slight warming, but satellite data showed a slight cooling.

Then in 1998, two scientists discovered the satellites had dropped in altitude, causing incorrect temperature readings. When the data was adjusted, it, too, showed a warming.

Now most scientists are talking about how big global warming will be and what it will mean.

Predictions range from a worldwide temperature rise of 2 to 6 degrees

Fahrenheit over the next 100 years.

That may not sound like much. "But it's likely it will mean changes in weather, and the changes are difficult to predict," says Jim Teeri, a University of Michigan biologist.

As it gets warmer, more water will evaporate, or be drawn out of the oceans and other bodies of water, as well as soil and plants. This could cause more droughts, or dry spells, killing crops and creating food shortages.

The warming may also cause glaciers and polar ice to melt, raising sea levels by one to two feet, says Teeri. That would cause major coastal flooding around the world. Some islands could disappear.

Scientists say we can't do much to stop global warming in the next 100 years. But we can prevent further warming in the 22nd Century — if we sharply cut CO_2 emissions now.

It won't be easy. CO_2 is formed by burning fossil fuels: oil, coal and gas. We use these every day to drive cars and tractors, fly planes, heat homes, run factories. The United States releases more CO_2 than any other country.

Trees and other plants remove CO_2 from the atmosphere but they can't remove it all and we're cutting down forests at an alarming rate.

"We are facing the most important challenge in the history of our species," says Teeri. "The challenge is to figure out how to manage the Earth wisely. All humans are going to have to be involved in solving these problems — and I mean everybody on the planet."

By Patricia Chargot

WHAT YOU CAN DO:

✪ Take action. Have your family join a car pool if you can. The fewer cars on the road, the less CO_2 in the atmosphere. Take a train instead of traveling long distances by car. Walk or ride your bike when you can.

Photo by Per Kjeldsen

The Yak travels the world, learning about the environmental challenges we face.

PEACE IS THE WAY TO A HAPPY FUTURE

Yak's Corner panelists agreed: Peace is a goal for the new millennium. From left, Domenic Terenzi, Megan Wampler, the Yak, Sam Wolson, Bobby McGibbon and Alexandra Sims are united in goals for the millennium.

Photo by Karin Anderson

When you make peace with someone, don't let it be a "cold" peace. Real peace means sharing and being interested in other people. Open your heart! Make peace warm.

The United Nations has declared 2000 as the International Year for the Culture of Peace. That means the UN's 185 member countries think teaching people how to solve conflicts by listening to each other will be very important in the 21st Century.

Obviously, it will be up to each of us to create peace in ourselves and others. But there already are hundreds of specially trained peace teachers in 70 countries, says Elise Boulding, a peace writer and lecturer.

"Ideally, during that first decade, an intensive program of teaching kids about peace will be launched all over the world," says Boulding, who helped set up the network of peace teachers and researchers in 1965.

"We'll be teaching peace in classrooms in the first grade. Every year, kids will learn more about how to deal with conflict without fighting or being violent.

By the time kids are in the sixth grade, they'll be very good at this and begin to teach their parents how to be more peaceful."

The Yak hopes Boulding's dream comes true.

Humans can be the friendliest creatures on the planet. But they can also be the meanest — wars and fighting have been around as long as humans have.

But in the 20th Century, war and fighting became a lot scarier with the development of high-powered guns and chemical, biological and nuclear weapons.

Photo by Hugh Grannum

Alex Dickinson, left, and Jim Glotzhober have shared ideas with the Yak on getting along. Says Alex, "Try to talk it out! If you can't solve a problem, talk to a teacher or an older person." Says Jim, "If you really don't like each other, you should stay away from each other. Otherwise, just try to be friends."

The United States and Russia alone have thousands of nuclear weapons — enough to destroy all of civilization. In 1998, India and Pakistan tested nuclear weapons for the first time, and other countries are expected to test them in the future.

Many people think nuclear weapons should be destroyed to make the world safer. Others think they're the best way for a country to protect itself — by scaring its neighbors. The countries that have them say they don't want to use them.

But the knowledge, ingredients and parts to make nuclear, biological and chemical weapons are spreading. Everyone hopes they don't get into the hands of terrorists, or people who use violence to terrify others.

Terrorists have bombed the U.S. embassies in Kenya and Tanzania in Africa and a Planet Hollywood in South Africa. U.S. Secretary of State Madeleine Albright calls terrorism "the war of the future."

Richard Chasdi, a terrorism expert, agrees.

"But this is not a Chicken Little situation," he says. "The sky is not going to fall. We should be concerned, but not panicked."

Chasdi says governments are working together more closely than ever to improve security and prevent terrorism.

Everyone can help by trying to be more sensitive to other cultures.

"Ask yourself, 'Why are people so angry at us around the world?' " says Chasdi. "A lot of people think the United States wants to dominate culturally. They think Americans just want to step on people."

As you travel and meet people from other cultures, try to listen and understand. Let them know you respect their traditions.

Remember: Peace begins with you.

By Patricia Chargot

WHAT KIDS CAN DO:

✪ Instead of renting an American movie, rent a film or cartoon from another country. It's a great way to learn about other cultures. How do the characters interact with each other? Do they act like the people in your family? We all share common concerns. Everyone cares about their families and the future.

✪ Learn a foreign language. It's a great way to appreciate another culture and it will open your mind in ways you can't imagine. So is listening to music from other countries. Check out CDs of ethnic music at the library. Play the music for your family and friends.

WHAT KIDS CAN DO:

✪ Make it your business to learn about the world and what's going on around you by reading newspapers and magazines.

✪ Get involved in politics — at school and in your community. Start by working on a campaign to improve your school or helping in local elections. A lot of adults are cynical about politics, but it's one of the best ways to change things you don't like. "Politics in the 21st Century will need an injection of enthusiasm, the highest dose possible," says Chasdi.

✪ Decide never to be a bully, hit others or use violence to get your way. These are not ways to solve problems. They just make the world an ugly place.

Photo by Hugh Grannum

The Yak heads into school with some pals who gave him great ideas on getting along together.

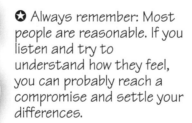

✪ Always remember: Most people are reasonable. If you listen and try to understand how they feel, you can probably reach a compromise and settle your differences.

✪ If you can't reach a compromise, ask a third person for help — a parent or a teacher. Pick someone you both trust and respect.

✪ Think about becoming a peace teacher or negotiator. Many colleges and universities have special programs.

The dove is a symbol of peace for many people.

What symbol would you choose to represent peace?

DOT TO DOT

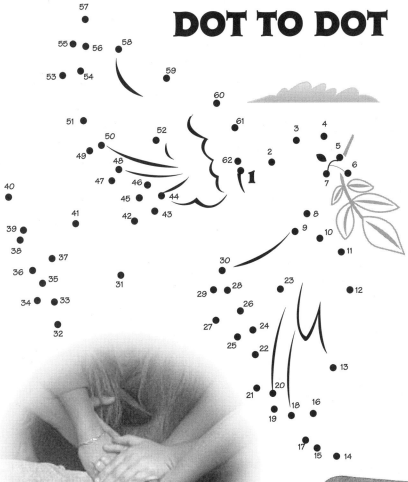

MAKE A PEACE BOARD

ere's an idea for school. Now that you've read some thoughts about making peace in the new millennium, share this idea with your class. Stories about conflict are in the news every day. See if you can find stories about people or countries that have resolved their differences, signed treaties or made a peace agreement. Make a peace bulletin board showing what was accomplished.

Always remember: Most people are reasonable. If you listen and try to understand how they feel, you probably can reach a compromise and settle your differences.

REMEMBER THE DINOSAURS? IT'S HAPPENING AGAIN

Gray wolf

"What's happening now is, we're going into this very high rate of extinction in the middle of a recovery period."
— Biologist Don Melnick

The bald eagle and the gray wolf are back! After nearly going extinct in the wild, these two beautiful animals and 14 others are expected to fly, leap and swim off the U.S. endangered list in the next few years.

But many species are still in trouble, from tiny bugs to the largest mammals.

Many frogs and other amphibians are disappearing, and scientists don't know why. Fish populations across the world are on the verge of collapse.

"Globally, probably 100 to 200 major fish species are being fished down to near extinction," says Kerry Bruce Clark, a biologist at Florida Institute of Technology.

"We used to feed on top carnivores, like tuna — great big fish that are easy to catch and feed a lot of people. You can still catch those fish, but there aren't as many.

"The average fish we're catching now is lower in the food chain — it's smaller and feeds closer to algae."

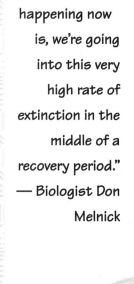

Scientists say species are always going extinct, but usually at a much slower pace. Large extinctions occur only every 20 million to 25 million years. Then the number of species gradually builds back up.

"What's happening now is, we're going into this very high rate of extinction in the middle of a recovery period," says Don Melnick, a biologist at Columbia University in New York.

"That's what everyone is worried about. Most scientists would suggest it will be greater than what occurred during the dinosaur die-off about 70 million years ago."

Yikes! No one knows for sure why the dinos disappeared, but humans didn't have anything to do with it — they didn't exist.

Since then, our species, Homo sapiens, has evolved and spread from Africa to every corner of the Earth, leaving its mark on many environments through building, hunting and pollution.

"This time, the extinction is man-made," says Melnick. "We've reduced the chances that many species will be able to survive over the long term."

Melnick and many other scientists say the mass extinction will occur over the next 50 years — unless humans act now. Can we do it? Can we save the black rhino, the giant panda, the tiger, the green-cheeked parrot?

Many groups around the world are trying. For example, U.S. and Canadian zoos and aquariums are trying to save more than 70 species, including mammals, birds, reptiles, amphibians and fish.

But almost all the animals that are expected to go extinct are ones that hardly anyone has heard of — tiny tropical arthropods, nematodes, bugs and worms. Michael Soule, an environmental scientist at the University of California, says these animals may account for more than 95 percent of the extinctions.

Scientists only recently discovered there may be TENS OF MILLIONS of species. Most people probably wouldn't even consider them animals, let alone get upset by their disappearance.

"But they're extremely important," says Melnick.

Microorganisms and insects transport nutrients from the soil to plants, and are food for lizards, birds, bats and other mammals. If they disappear, so will many tropical plants and animals. Some tropical birds could stop migrating to the United States, where they may play a critical role in a particular environment.

"We just don't know," says Clark.

What we do know, scientists say, is that we are all linked in ways we are just beginning to understand.

By Patricia Chargot

Bald eagles

"Globally, probably 100 to 200 major fish species are being fished down to near extinction."
— Biologist Kerry Bruce Clark

WHAT YOU CAN DO

✪ Help save endangered animals in your area. It's great to support groups such as the World Wildlife Fund, but there may be a patch of habitat in your own backyard that needs protecting! You or your family can join a local conservation group.

Photo by David P. Gilkey

The awesome peregrine falcon was removed from the U.S. endangered list in August, but it's still endangered in many states.

✪ Learn all you can about the animal world. Visit the World Wildlife Fund's Web site at **www.worldwildlife.org**. And read about animals in books and newspapers. But don't stop there! Get to know real animals by visiting zoos and aquariums and taking nature walks. Ask your local zoo or aquarium which species it is actively involved in trying to save, and see what you can do to help. For example, the Louisville Zoological Garden manages the program to save the Cuban crocodile, which now lives only in two small swamps in Cuba. The zoo is trying to raise money to teach Cuban kids about their little-known crocodilian treasure. Learning about an animal is the first step toward caring about its survival.

✪ Consider becoming an environmental scientist. "We need many more than we have now," says Melnick, director of Columbia's Center for Environmental Research and Conservation. (Visit the center's Web site at **cerc.columbia.edu**.)

"We need the best people, as far as I'm concerned. This is like the space race — we're going to need the best minds. The greatest issue we all face is, 'What is our environment going to

Overfishing is threatening many fish species. One cause is overly large fishing nets, such as this one. Stretched out, it would cover 15 soccer fields.

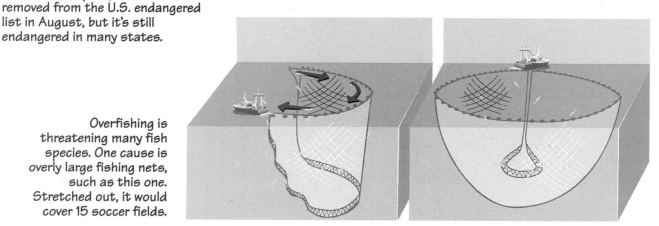

Graphic by Martha Thierry/KRT

Learn all you can about the animal world from alligators to zebras.

Can we save the black rhino, the giant panda, the tiger, the green-cheeked parrot?

look like 100 years from now and can we survive that kind of transformation? And if not, what are we going to do about it and who is going to do it?' "

✪ Listen to what other people have to say about the environment — even if you don't agree with them. Many people are struggling to find a balance between protecting animals and protecting "property rights" — the right of people to use their land any way they want. Should people be allowed to destroy animal and plant habitats to build things like homes and shopping centers? Under what conditions?

✪ Learn all you can about the U.S. Endangered Species Act, which is more than 25 years old. Write your U.S. senators and representatives and let them know how you feel about any proposed changes — before they become law.

PLANTS NEED OUR HELP, TOO

Photo by Edward Voss

Human development threatens plants of the Great Lakes shoreline, including the pitcher's thistle, above, and the dwarf lake iris, left.

Half of all plants live in tropical forests, which take up only six to seven percent of the Earth's land.

That's pretty amazing. It's also scary because humans are destroying tropical forests at an alarming rate. Scientists say that many tropical plants are on the verge of extinction.

"At least a quarter of all tropical plant species will be gone before too long in the next millennium," says Anton Reznicek, a botanist at the University of Michigan.

"I'm inclined to suspect it could be much higher than that."

How many species is Reznicek talking about? There are about 250,000 plant species on Earth, including trees, flowers, grasses, bushes and weeds. About half, or 125,000 species, live in tropical forests; so a quarter of those — more than 31,000 plant species — are expected to disappear.

Yikes! This news upset the Yak, who loves plants and, of course, is a herbivore, or vegetarian.

"But you must never be pessimistic because there's always something to save," says Reznicek, who travels all over the world to collect plant specimens for U-M's Herbarium, or plant library.

"The harder we work to save as much as possible, the better life will be in the 21st and 22nd centuries."

The main problem is deforestation, or the clearing of forests for lumber, cattle ranches, farming, mining and new highways, towns and

"The harder we work to save as much as possible, the better life will be in the 21st and 22nd centuries."

— Botanist Anton Reznicek

cities. Many forests were cut down in the 19th and 20th centuries, too. But they were mainly in the temperate zone, the part of the planet between the tropics and the arctic and antarctic circles. The temperate zone includes North America.

"We lost plants, but not as many," says Reznicek. "Our impact on the globe wasn't as severe."

That's because many plants in the temperate zone are widespread, or grow across large areas — say from Maine to Minnesota. If you destroy a plant in one area, you can probably find it elsewhere.

But the closer you get to the equator, the smaller a plant's range is, and that makes it more vulnerable to extinction.

"It's the nature of life," says Reznicek. "But you can't ask or order people in the tropics not to do what we did — so education is important."

People all over the world have to learn how important plants and trees are so we stop destroying them, he says.

Plants are a main source of food for both humans and animals. Many also produce chemical compounds that are used by shamans, or tribal doctors, to treat diseases. Some rain forest medicines, such as quinine, have saved thousands of lives all over the world. Quinine (KWI-nine) is used to treat malaria, a disease carried by mosquitoes.

"When the forests come down, whole libraries of information will come down, too," says Larry Davenport, a botanist at Samford University in Birmingham, Alabama.

"And the shamans, the folks with the best knowledge of plants, are dying off. The younger people are not as interested. It's very rare anymore to meet a 30-year-old shaman."

Davenport, who visits the rain forest every year, says he and other botanists are "frantic" to learn all they can before the plants and shamans disappear.

"We're rookies as far as knowledge of tropical plants is concerned," he says.

Forests also absorb massive amounts of carbon dioxide — called CO_2 — from the atmosphere, which helps control global warming. Tropical forests are like huge CO_2 sponges that help support life on the whole planet!

Now, they need our support, too.

By Patricia Chargot

> "When the forests come down, whole libraries of information will come down, too," says
> — Botanist Larry Davenport

Photo by Andrew Johnston

Flowering marsh marigolds.

■ The 250,000 plant species do not include what scientists call the lower plant species, such as algae, fungi and mosses, which don't have internal structures for transporting liquids.

WHAT YOU CAN DO:

✪ Get involved in environmental programs of all kinds, not just recycling programs but also cleanup and protection programs. Find out what plant species are threatened in your area and do what you can to save them.

✪ Learn the names of the trees and plants in your region. Knowing the names of living things is the first step toward caring about them.

✪ Consider a career that's related to the natural world. Become a botanist, biologist or ecologist.

✪ Learn to love the natural world — plants, animals, forests, lakes and oceans. "It's easy to sit in front of a TV or computer and see the impact of science, but it doesn't really make people care," says botanist Anton Reznicek. Visit nature areas, parks and farms as often as you can.

Devil's club, above, can be found in northwestern North America and the Great Lakes region, including parts of Canada and Michigan's Isle Royale National Park. Listed as threatened, this sharp, spiny plant may be vulnerable to global warming. Why is it called devil's club? Because it can cut you!

"You must never be pessimistic because there's always something to save."

— Botanist Anton Reznicek

Photo by Greg Johnstone

The Yak visits a cherry orchard.

PLANT A TREE

✪ Check with your school principal to see if you can help make your playground a greener place to play. See if your local garden store will donate a tree. Then research what tree type grows best in your area. If you can get a free tree, work out a planting day. You can track the tree's growth as you go through school!

MAKE A CHILDREN'S GARDEN

✪ There are often corners in your yard, park or school playground that would be ripe for a garden. See if one area can be marked off for kids to use. Easy-to-grow plants like sunflowers are something you can plant in the spring — then come back in the fall and see how they've grown tall. You can also plant bulbs in the fall — tulips are the Yak's favorite. Just wait until spring and your garden will be filled with color.

BE A NATURE SCOUT!

✪ You don't have to travel far to explore nature. Your own backyard or a nearby park has plenty to see and do. Take a notebook with you and draw some of the things you see. Take a small bag to make a collection of rocks, nuts, leaves and pine cones. Later, you could use some of your natural treasures to create crafts.

A SYMBOL OF YOUR STATE

✪ Does your state have a state plant, flower or tree? If it does, research it. Is there another symbol your state still hasn't adopted (such as a wildflower or state insect or even state fungus)?

Photo by Per Kjeldsen

The Yak is off on another adventure.

MAKE A WISH LIST

What are your wishes for the new millennium? We yakked with elementary school kids about their wishes for the future.

What are they?

Domenic Terenzi says we need to colonize space. Domenic figures that would solve a lot of problems of overcrowding and make for a peaceful world if we all had more room.

Alexandra Sims doesn't know yet if she wants to be president, but her wish is that people would elect someone who would bring more diversity to the White House.

Sam Wolson really gets bugged about advertisements for toys that aren't good. He's also tired of politicians who make promises they don't keep and politicians who don't tell the truth.

Bobby McGibbon says stopping pollution is truly important.

For Megan Wampler, all those goals are fine ones, but she'd like to see a ban on all drugs. She'd like to live in a world with no smoking and no harmful drugs.

What are your wishes?

Take some time to really think about the future. We are living in an amazing time, but it's also a little scary. What are your hopes and dreams? Turn to the Millennium Journal in this book to fill in your wishes.

COLONIZE SPACE

DIVERSITY IN THE WHITE HOUSE

STOP POLLUTION

BAN DRUGS

TELL THE TRUTH

Our Yak panelists shared their goals with us. From left, Domenic Terenzi, Alexandra Sims, Sam Wolson, Bobby McGibbon and Megan Wampler. They think kids will be able to make changes. What do you think?

READ YOUR WAY INTO THE FUTURE

The millennium is a great time to make yourself an imagination station: a cozy corner where you can curl up with a great book. Writers have always loved imagining the future — or what it would be like to travel through space and time! Here are some fun books to read right through the millennium.

FOR EARLY READERS:

"**June 29, 1999**" by David Wiesner. What happens when you experiment and get giant vegetables?

"**Rachel Field's Hitty, Her First Hundred Years,**" adapted by Rosemary Wells and illustrated by Susan Jeffers. Your grandmother probably loved this book about Hitty, the little carved doll who travels through 100 years of adventures.

"**My Robot Buddy**" by Alfred Slote. For his 10th birthday, Jack asks for a robot so he can have someone to play with.

FOR MIDDLE READERS:

"**It's All Greek to Me**" by Jon Scieszka. The Time Warp trio travel back in time to meet the Greek gods and goddesses.

"**Tuck Everlasting**" by Natalie Babbitt. The Tuck family has a spring whose water allows them to live forever. Is that good or bad?

"**The Phantom Tollbooth**" by Norton Juster. Milo drives through a tollbooth and ends up in a magical land. Watch out for Mountains of Ignorance.

"**A Wrinkle in Time**" by Madeleine L'Engle. Meg and her brother set out to find their father who's trapped in time.

"**Willie Bea and the Time the Martians Landed**" by Virginia Hamilton. In October 1938, Willie Bea thinks the Martians have landed when "The War of the Worlds" is broadcast on radio.

Photo by Gabriel B. Tait

FOR OLDER READERS:

"**The Martian Chronicles**" by Ray Bradbury. What if we had a space colony on Mars?

"**Fahrenheit 451**" by Ray Bradbury. Imagine a world where owning a book is a crime.

SERIES BOOKS:

"**Animorphs**" books by K.A. Applegate are filled with weird science. Plus, it's fun to imagine morphing into a tiger or a bird.

And, of course, the popular "**Harry Potter**" books, by J.K. Rowling, are great fantasy.

By Cathy Collison

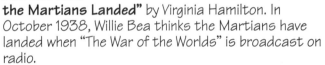

TRAVEL WITH THE YAK BACK IN TIME

BE A TIME TRACKER

Many of you have made a personal timeline at school. That timeline charts the important events in your life. But the millennium is a perfect time to make a timeline going back 1,000 years.

Whew! That sounds like a big task, but we can help you out. Take a look at this timeline. A timeline can contain as little or as much information as you like. The Yak timeline is a mix of important dates and just plain interesting ones. We only had a small space, but you could make a grand timeline by charting one down a school hallway.

If you're really ambitious, you can make one based on what MIGHT happen in the next 1,000 years. We've just touched the surface. Go ahead, travel through time. We hope traveling back will make it easier to travel forward.

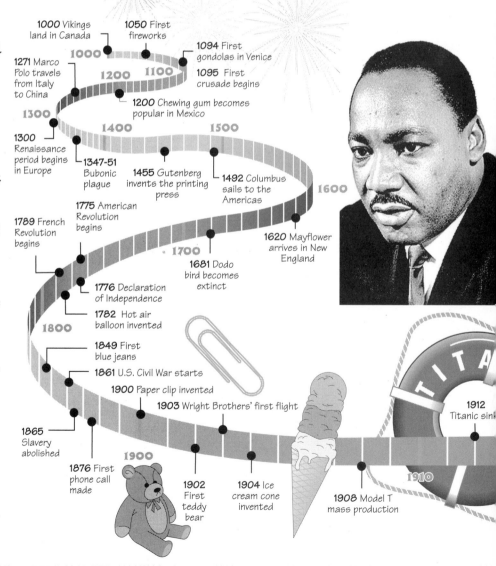

1000 Vikings land in Canada

1050 First fireworks

1094 First gondolas in Venice

1095 First crusade begins

1271 Marco Polo travels from Italy to China

1200 Chewing gum becomes popular in Mexico

1300 Renaissance period begins in Europe

1347-51 Bubonic plague

1455 Gutenberg invents the printing press

1492 Columbus sails to the Americas

1620 Mayflower arrives in New England

1681 Dodo bird becomes extinct

1775 American Revolution begins

1789 French Revolution begins

1776 Declaration of Independence

1782 Hot air balloon invented

1849 First blue jeans

1861 U.S. Civil War starts

1900 Paper clip invented

1903 Wright Brothers' first flight

1865 Slavery abolished

1876 First phone call made

1902 First teddy bear

1904 Ice cream cone invented

1908 Model T mass production

1912 Titanic sinks

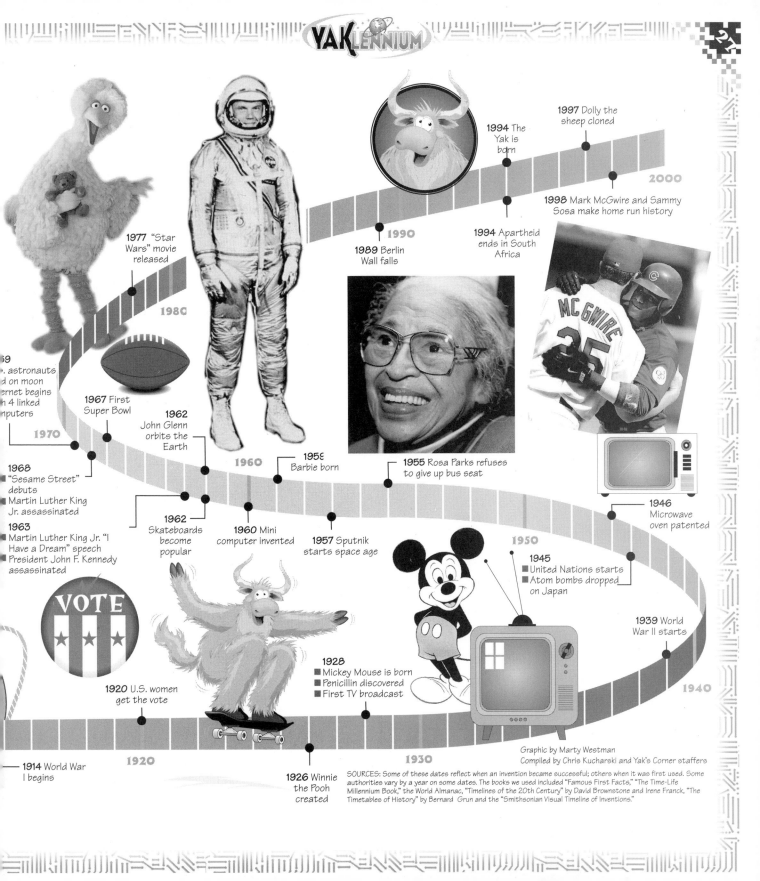

1997 Dolly the sheep cloned

1994 The Yak is born

1998 Mark McGwire and Sammy Sosa make home run history

2000

1994 Apartheid ends in South Africa

1990

1989 Berlin Wall falls

1977 "Star Wars" movie released

1980

1946 Microwave oven patented

1955 Rosa Parks refuses to give up bus seat

1950

1967 First Super Bowl

1962 John Glenn orbits the Earth

1959 Barbie born

1960

69 astronauts d on moon ernet begins h 4 linked puters

1970

1968
"Sesame Street" debuts
Martin Luther King Jr. assassinated

1963
Martin Luther King Jr. "I Have a Dream" speech
President John F. Kennedy assassinated

1962 Skateboards become popular

1960 Mini computer invented

1957 Sputnik starts space age

1945
United Nations starts
Atom bombs dropped on Japan

1939 World War II starts

VOTE

1920 U.S. women get the vote

1928
Mickey Mouse is born
Penicillin discovered
First TV broadcast

1940

1914 World War I begins

1920

1926 Winnie the Pooh created

1930

Graphic by Marty Westman
Compiled by Chris Kucharski and Yak's Corner staffers

SOURCES: Some of these dates reflect when an invention became successful; others when it was first used. Some authorities vary by a year on some dates. The books we used included "Famous First Facts," "The Time-Life Millennium Book," the World Almanac, "Timelines of the 20th Century" by David Brownstone and Irene Franck, "The Timetables of History" by Bernard Grun and the "Smithsonian Visual Timeline of Inventions."

COMPUTERS, CAFES AND LEARNING ALL YEAR

Most Yak's Corner readers will be graduating from high school by the year 2010. So here's a pop quiz for all of you millennium grads:

What will school be like in the new millennium? (Circle the best answer.)
A. You'll be able to choose the school you attend.
B. Your school will be loaded with computers — you'll probably have one in every classroom.
C. You'll take summer school classes on the Web.
D. Your school cafeteria will serve the best food you've ever tasted.

OK, we tossed the last answer in to see if you were paying attention.

There's a good bet that A, B, and C will be true for most students in the near future, says Kathy Christie of the Education Commission of the States, an organization that works with state leaders to make schools better.

Many politicians, including President Bill Clinton, have been talking a lot about the need for more choices in public schools. Schools with alternative — or non-traditional —

Students at Coyote Canyon Elementary School in Rancho Cucamonga, California, help set up a courtyard like a Native American village.

calendars will be options too.

Dr. Charles Ballinger of the National Association for Year-Round Education hopes that in the next 30 years all schools will become year-round.

President Clinton wants every classroom in America to be linked to the Internet by the new millennium, and there's a good chance that will happen.

"We're rapidly seeing computers installed in classrooms and classrooms getting wired," says Tom Bird, an associate professor of education at Michigan State University. "And computers are getting less and less expensive,

---

New schools will have more friendly spaces. You won't get "shhhhed" in libraries of the future because they will have reading areas and talking areas.

so schools can get more."

One creative way schools will use computers is to offer classes on the Web.

And what will the schools of the future look like?

Architect Gaylaird Christopher, who heads the Los Angeles office of Perkins & Will, an architectural firm that builds schools all over the world, says he often talks to kids about what they want their schools to look like.

"More and more, educators are involving students in the planning process of building new schools," he says. One thing students say over and over is to "make it real," says Christopher. Students want "hands-on areas where they can get messy and dirty working on art projects and science experiments."

The solution: New schools will have more sinks in the classrooms for quick cleanups. They will also have more student-friendly spaces. For example, you won't get "shhhhed" in libraries of the future because they will have reading areas and talking areas. High school libraries probably will have cafe-type areas where students can get a drink and snack, just as your favorite bookstores do now.

Classrooms will look different too:

Expect future schools to have cafes and cozy reading spaces.

There will be areas to work in groups or alone, and areas for class presentations. For plays and concerts, schools will have large theaters.

Christopher predicts that classrooms will be expanded to include the community. Even grade school and middle school students will be reaching out to local businesses, serving apprenticeships or spending more time out of the classroom on community field trips.

Professor Bird and Kathy Christie say it's hard to predict exactly what will happen. A lot will depend on students, parents and voters to support schools and figure out what works best for each school district.

"It will be what we make it," says Professor Bird. The Yak hopes parents, teachers and local governments make schools safe and exciting for every student — and yummy cafeteria food would be nice, too.

By Janis Campbell

Photos by Mary Schroeder

Year-round school is already happening across the country. In the future, more and more kids, like these students at Vandenberg School in Southfield, Michigan, will attend classes year-round.

GO BACK IN TIME

Interview your grandparents or other older relatives about what school was like when they were young. Then head to the library and research even earlier times — especially school at the last turn-of-the century. Plan an old-fashioned school day for your room. Play games, read stories and have a lunch that kids might have eaten in the 1890s.

YOUR SCHOOL HISTORY

Check out your own school history. Old or new, it still has a story. See if you can find out how the land was used before a school was built there. Talk to people who went to school when it first opened. Are there any famous graduates?

DESIGN A DREAM SCHOOL

Make a wish list for your dream school. What would you put in it? What resources should it have? Do some research at the library using newspapers, magazines and the Internet. Find out about modern schools. Draw a design of your future school and write a short description on what needs to be included.

MILLENNIUM SWAP MEET

There's no time like a millennium to clean your closets! Gather your old toys and games and set aside a day in the gym where kids can have tables of stuff to sell or swap. All the money collected can go to buy something for your school.

Photo by William Archie

The Yak wonders: What will a school bus of the future be like? Will it fly? Will it be a different color than yellow? Design your bus of the future.

COMPUTERS WILL BE TINY— BUT SMARTER

You probably use a computer at home or at school. What are computers going to look like in five or 10 years?

Nothing like they do now. We asked some people working on the next generation of PCs to tell us what they think is in store. **Hint:** Think TINY.

Betsy Riley, assistant to the director of the computer science department at Oak Ridge Nuclear Laboratory in Tennessee, is testing tomorrow's computers today. Riley thinks the next few years will bring great new toys that learn what you teach them and can do tricks, using tiny computers inside. She says it'll be like the movie "Small Soldiers," but without the guns.

Kids could be carrying around tiny communications computers on their wrists. These could have a pager, cellular phone, locator and even a biosensor (which could take your temperature and check your health). Your mom could use the pager to call you to dinner, check the locator to see where you were and the biosensor to make sure you were OK.

Right now, Riley says, scientists are experimenting with a flexible sheet that looks like plastic that can display computer pictures just like a monitor. Riley says the next step after that is easy: building it into clothes.

You could get up in the morning and type in

what you wanted your T-shirt or your hat to say.

Judi Moline, a computer scientist, says she sees a time when you won't be looking at computer screens. Instead, the wall of your classroom — or even your living room — could be a screen.

Computers would be mostly voice-controlled, she thinks, and could recognize when you walked into the room and turn on by themselves.

So with all this new technology, have you missed your chance to become the next Bill Gates? No way, says Amy Bruckman, assistant professor of computing at Georgia Institute of Technology. She's working on a project now to help today's kids be part of the next generation of computer stars.

At her Web site, kids can learn how to do easy computer programming, including making virtual pets. To get more information, visit **www.cc.gatech.edu/~asb/ moose-crossing**

By Heather Newman

The next few years will bring great new toys that learn what you teach them and can do tricks, using tiny computers inside.

TALK TO YOUR CAR— AND TAKE A TRAIN

This GM Sunraycer is an experimental car that operates on solar power.

You say to your dashboard: "Hey, Waldo, would you check my E-mail? If I have any, would you read it? Then, would you please call home?"

The year is 2010. You have just finished college and are driving to a new city in your first new car.

You say to your dashboard: "Hey, Waldo, would you check my E-mail? If I have any, would you read it? Then, would you please call home?"

Waldo, a voice-activated computer, reads three electronic messages out loud. Then he dials your home phone number so you can talk to your roomie and say hi to your dog.

Whoa! Will driving in the 21st Century be cool or what?

"Talking to your dashboard is maybe five to 10 years away," says Scott Fosgard, a spokesman for Chrysler Corporation.

The Yak interviewed Fosgard at a "Convergence" conference in Dearborn, Michigan. It was a convergence, or coming together, of hundreds of technologists from two industries: automotive and electronics.

The goal was to share information and take electronics to the "next step" in cars and trucks. People were talking about all kinds of cool things, such as a portable cell phone with a computer screen to show you the fastest, safest way to get somewhere.

(Electronic navigation systems for cars already exist, but they cost about $2,500; a portable system might cost as little as $250.)

Most importantly, the 21st Century will bring new kinds of cars that could change life on Earth — for the better.

Auto companies are racing to develop cars that use cleaner energy sources and fuels, such as electric batteries, fuel cells, hydrogen and methanol.

The cars will emit much less carbon dioxide, or CO_2, and other pollutants than gasoline-fueled cars with internal combustion engines — the kind most people drive now.

General Motors Corporation already is leasing 600 electric cars in California and Arizona. There are still problems to solve — the cars must be recharged every 70 to 90 miles. But the company plans soon to unveil a car that will run for 150 miles before it needs recharging.

Meanwhile, Ford Motor Company is testing the P2000 HFC, a fuel cell car that uses hydrogen.

A fuel cell is like a battery, but it doesn't store energy. It uses hydrogen to produce electricity, which is what powers the car. The energy is produced as it is needed, so the cell doesn't have to be recharged, which takes a long time. But it does have to be refueled — with hydrogen, a completely clean, or "zero emission" fuel.

(You can use methanol and gasoline in a fuel cell, too, but there will be some emissions.)

Ford plans to start selling the new cars by 2004.

But in the 21st Century, many customers might not even want to drive cars as much as they do today.

Some transportation experts say new, faster trains and subways will be built and more of us will ride them.

"I think there will be a renaissance in rail traffic in the the United States," says David Gosling of the University of Cincinnati.

"Cars will be used for very short journeys, maybe to drive 100 miles a day."

Germany, Japan and France are leading the way, but U.S. companies are building modern trains, too, says Gosling. He says he was "astonished" two years ago to find a state-of-the-art subway in Singapore in Asia. The system was completely computer controlled.

"As I was getting off, I looked up and saw a sign that said, 'Made in the U.S. by Westinghouse.' What's wrong with this country? We're in the forefront of technology, but we don't seem to understand the importance of new forms of transportation."

Not all experts are as optimistic.

Patricia Waller, a transportation expert at the University of Michigan, says Americans probably will be more dependent on cars than ever in the new millennium.

The reason is, we're building more houses outside towns and cities — instead of near future train lines.

And gasoline is still much cheaper in the United States than in most other countries. There's no incentive, or reward, for not driving cars.

"Unless the kids coming along today understand the connections between having a big house in the country, driving back and forth as much as you want in a gas guzzler, and the air we breathe," nothing will change, says Waller.

Now, do you really want to drive your first new car to that new city? Or do you want to take the train?

By Patricia Chargot

Ford's P2000 HFC

Photo by Mary Schroeder

The Yak is ready to fuel the P2000 with hydrogen!

IT'S FAST, IT'S FUN, IT'S GLOBAL

As the Hispanic population increases in the United States, we'll continue to have more Hispanic-style flavors in all our dishes. In fact, we'll have lots of global goodies.

The new millennium will be good news for picky eaters. You won't have to pick at your food — you'll be able to pick more food.

How so?

We'll be eating more vegetables — or food that may resemble meat but is made of vegetables like soybeans. And we'll have many more choices of dishes to reflect individual tastes or heritages. Delane Myers, an associate professor in foods at Iowa State University, has been studying what people want in food. And what they want is convenience — easy and fast to serve — but also choice.

To increase convenience, scientists will be working to make microwave cooking even faster. We'll also have home-style food to pick up and carry home from stores and restaurants. The deli sections of your grocery store may keep growing.

New packaging also may cut down preparation time. Already we have salads chopped and washed and in bags. There will likely be more boxing of vegetables and fruits, sliced and diced. People will take them and prepare a fresh meal.

And we'll have food that can stay in the refrigerator before it's zapped, not just the freezer. That means less time to heat up.

Is there a down side to food development? Even now, some microwave dishes have high sodium (salt) content.

People will need to watch labels closely and decide if they want some of the ingredients that are used to make food taste good when it's cooked quickly.

People are trying to grow foods differently by developing hybrids that keep flavor and ship well. They do this with genetic engineering, changing the food's genes. This can be good; crops can be changed to fight plant diseases, or they can actually help people with food allergies or illnesses. But we can't predict all the effects, so it's important to be alert to changes and find out how food is grown.

Some people want food with no

additives at all. So there is likely to be an expansion of organic farming, which grows crops and raises livestock without any additives, chemicals and pesticides.

In the best of future food worlds, choice will extend to health needs. For instance, people who are allergic to wheat can't eat wheat bread. But scientists are developing substitutes that make good-tasting alternatives.

Does any of this mean the end of traditional big family meals like Thanksgiving? No, says Dr. Myers. But it could mean you'll bring more of that food in — already people pick up a pie or dessert at a restaurant, or even a whole dinner. Your family may choose to eat out that day, or just make one special family dish. That dish could be chicken mole or soba (Japanese noodles) or soybean burgers.

And maybe you'll be the cook yourself. Now that's out of this world.

By Cathy Collison

WHAT YOU CAN DO

✪ Scientists predict we'll be eating a larger variety of food in the future. Head to the library and check out cookbooks for kids. Find some recipes that don't take long to make — but are new and different for your family.

✪ As you explore foods of the future, you will need to make careful choices. Look closely at labels. Watch for high sugar, fat or salt. Learn what's in the foods you eat. If it doesn't have ingredients that are healthy, don't buy it.

✪ Read reviews of restaurants. See if you can learn about ethnic restaurants that serve food from other countries.

お子様ランチ
Lunch for kid
800円

French fries, yogurt, veggies, hamburger and shrimp: These small portions are all part of a department store lunch for Japanese children. A variety of different foods in small portions could be more common everywhere soon.

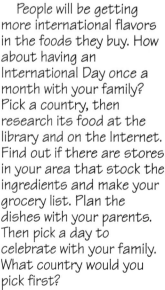

A TASTE OF TOMORROW

You can have lots of fun with food: making menus, cooking and, of course, the best part — sampling the food. Here are some fun ideas to get you started.

BLEND INTO THE FUTURE

Will kids of the future still have milk mustaches? We predict they will, since milk will always be important for your body. But experts say kids will be drinking more exotic flavors of milk. Try making some smoothies for the millennium and do a taste test. With adult help, find your favorite smoothie recipe and substitute new ingredients for the ones you've already tried. Here are some fun starters: kiwi fruit, mango or coconut. You might want to research foods in the library before you blend.

GO GLOBAL

People will be getting more international flavors in the foods they buy. How about having an International Day once a month with your family? Pick a country, then research its food at the library and on the Internet. Find out if there are stores in your area that stock the ingredients and make your grocery list. Plan the dishes with your parents. Then pick a day to celebrate with your family. What country would you pick first?

SCHOOL LUNCH MENU, 2089

What would a school be serving for lunch way in the future? Design a menu for a week in the year 2089. This would be good for a class to do. Have fun with naming dishes and guessing how the cafeteria would look. (Will there still be trays? Will kids eat in special pods instead of at tables?)

INTERNATIONAL MIX

Here's another fun idea: Brainstorm up a snack, juice and other fixings for a lunch you'd want to pack in the new millennium. Lots of kids make trail mix, a healthy crunchy concoction, using a favorite snack mix. What else could you stir up? Take a trip to the grocery store and check out the dry snacks — but not just in the chips and cracker aisle. How about some Chinese noodles in your mix? Or tortilla chips with macadamia nuts? If you want, put travel stickers or some other global designs on your lunchbox.

MAKE IT FAST

Yep, we'll still be on the run in the new millennium. That means sometimes having to take food on the run — or doing something while we eat. A couple of years ago, people came up with carriers for water bottles for busy sports kids. Can you create a food or drink container for people on the go?

EAT LIKE AN ASTRONAUT

Want to eat like an astronaut? See if you can make your own space menu from this list of astronaut food. That's what astronauts do. About four months before a mission, they get to plan their own menus.

On the space shuttle, there are three basic kinds of food. One kind is called rehydratable. Astronauts add water. Another kind is called thermostabilized. It's heated in an oven in the shuttle's galley, or kitchen. What's the third kind? It's simple treats, like shiny red apples, crunchy cookies and flour tortillas, that can be eaten just the way they are.

None of the food is squeezed out of a tube anymore. Astronauts use a knife, fork and spoon to eat, just as you do. But they have an extra eating utensil: a scissors for cutting open food packages. And they never have to wash dishes. All the containers go right into the trash compactor.

Here are your menu choices for a space dinner:

By Marcy Abramson

APPETIZERS
Carrots and celery (but only on the first two days of a mission. After that, they spoil.)
Cream of mushroom soup
Shrimp cocktail

MAIN DISHES
Macaroni and cheese
Chicken and rice casserole
Steak
Spaghetti with meat sauce

VEGGIES
Asparagus
Broccoli with cheese sauce
Green beans with mushrooms

DESSERT
Brownies
Butter cookies
Chocolate, vanilla or butterscotch pudding

AFTER DINNER SNACK
Apple
Banana
Orange
Trail mix
Peanuts
Yogurt

DRINKS
Apple cider
Cherry, orange or grape drink
Cocoa
Lemonade
Tropical punch

MAKE YOUR RESERVATIONS FOR MARS

"Kids today will get to go to space. You'll be able to buy a ticket."
— Alan Ladwig, senior NASA adviser

In the next century, you'll be able to take a cruise in outer space and watch spectacular sunsets every 90 minutes. You — or your children — may live on the moon or a space station. Or, using virtual travel, you'll be there as probes explore the moons of Jupiter and beyond.

That's how NASA, the National Aeronautics and Space Administration, sees the future.

"Kids today will get to go to space," says Alan Ladwig, senior adviser to NASA administrator Daniel Goldin. "You'll be able to buy a ticket."

Already, he says, private companies are taking reservations for short flights to space. By the time you grow up, you'll be able to take space cruises in Earth orbit and visit space hotels.

You'll explore faraway space, too, through virtual reality. Within the next 10 years, you may be able to control a robot on the moon, Ladwig says. You'll be using a computer on Earth, of course, but you'll be able to cyber-drive right up and check out Neil Armstrong's footprints.

The next millennium of space exploration is well underway. Deep Space 1, a probe, and Deep Space 2, an unmanned lander, are heading for Mars. The Chandra X-Ray Observatory was put into orbit in 1999 by shuttle Columbia on the first NASA mission commanded by a woman, Lt. Col. Eileen Collins.

The Mars 2001 Lunar Lander is scheduled to launch on April 10, 2001. The unmanned mission will study the planet and look for landing sites for astronauts. You can send your name to Mars with it! To find out how, check out NASA's cool Web site for kids, **www.nasa.gov/kids.html.** There are already more than 700,000 names on the CD-ROM, but there's room for lots more. Names will be collected until December 2000.

Another probe, Cassini, will visit the moons of Saturn in 2004. Later in the new millennium, such probes will head even farther into outer space.

In 2007, the U.S. and Europe plan to build the Next Generation Space Telescope — the successor to the Hubble Space Telescope. It should send back dynamite pictures.

The International Space Station is now being built in space. The space station will be created by men and women from Europe, Russia, Canada, Japan and the United States working together.

Private companies are getting into space, too. Most are research and communications companies, but some are planning to start colonies on Mars and the moon. And others are travel agencies for space cruises!

The space race started in the 1950s as part of the Cold War between the United States and the Soviet Union. The two enemies were racing to try to control space. Today the two friends are partners in exploring space for the benefit of all people.

Now that's progress for a new millennium.

By Marcy Abramson

The space shuttle Discovery

The Hubble Space Telescope

WHAT TO DO

⊛ NASA for Kids has so many great activities on its Web site, you'll want to try them all. Here are some of the Yak's favorites:

✪ Send a space postcard to a friend for a birthday or just to celebrate a special accomplishment. You choose the picture and write the greeting.

✪ Like the Yak, NASA for Kids has a gallery of kids' art. You can send out-of-this-world artwork to **Becky Bray, E047, Marshall Space Flight Center, MSFC, AL 35812.**

✪ Have you always wanted to go to Space Camp? Maybe you can. Your class could organize a project to go and hold fund-raisers to help pay for it. Space Camp also has some scholarships to give out to individual students. Check it out at **www.spacecamp.com**

SPACE-AGE SCIENCE

All kinds of medical and scientific discoveries have been made through the space program — and there will be lots more in the next millennium.

Electric power, for example, may come from satellites collecting energy from the sun. Science fiction writers have had that idea for a long time; it could become reality by the end of the next century.

"A lot of science fiction becomes science fact," says NASA senior adviser Alan Ladwig.

The Deep Space 1 probe that was launched in October, 1998, is based on technology right out of "Star Trek" — it can think for itself and uses a new kind of power called ion propulsion.

"This is the first 'Star Trek'-y thing that NASA has done," says Curt Cleven, deputy spacecraft systems manager for Deep Space 1.

Unlike science fiction, however, NASA doesn't try to predict more than about 40 years into the future. "It's too hard to imagine the things that you can't imagine — the great leaps in scientific technology," says Ladwig. "We might be too conservative."

Smoke detectors, heart pacemakers and shock-absorbing sneakers all got their start in space technology.

Here are some other cool inventions that came from space technology:

✪ Communications satellites that bring us live TV from all over the world.

✪ Plastic sandwich wrap.

✪ Cordless tools.

✪ Signaling systems that warn porpoises away from deadly fishing nets.

✪ Ear thermometers.

This is a computer generated image of an experimental rocketship that could replace the shuttle.

COLONIZE SPACE

Domenic Terenzi thinks building a space colony would be a great millennium goal.

MAKE AN OUTER SPACE FRIEND

Imagine you find a new friend on your space travels. If you could take your new friend back to Earth, where would you take the alien? Write a story about your adventures with your alien buddy.

JOIN THE CLUB

Does your school have a chapter of the Young Astronauts Club? Ask your classroom teacher or science teacher about starting one. It's a national organization for kids who love space.

TO THE MOON!

A moon colony is being planned by a private group, called the Artemis Project, by the second decade of the 21st Century. Is this really possible? Check it out for yourself at the Artemis Web site, **www.asi.org**

TAKE A METEOR SHOWER

You can see some fireworks in the sky without leaving your home planet. Every year there are big meteor showers in August (the Perseids) and November (the Leonids). Check with a science museum or planetarium to find out the best day for viewing. You also can find tips about sky watching in your newspaper and on-line.

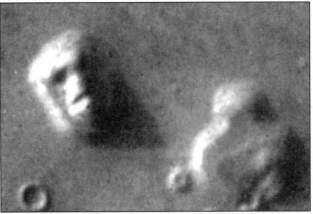

Photos courtesy of NASA

The rock formation on the left is called "The Face." This photo came from the Mars probe Viking two decades ago. What would you call it?

Here, the Mars surface is captured in 1997 by the Mars Pathfinder probe. Will you be able to travel to Mars someday? Maybe you will.

TRAVEL BACK TO THE LAST MILLENNIUM

Find out what life was like when 999 became 1000

One thousand years ago, anyone who reached the age of 10 was lucky.

Life was so hard in many parts of the world that children often died of disease, malnutrition, natural disasters or war.

There were some wonderfully exciting places to live in the world: the dazzling city of Cordoba in what is now Spain, the gold-rich kingdoms of Ghana and Great Zimbabwe in Africa, the amazing high-rise cities built along steep cliffs in the American Southwest by the Anasazi — and the beautiful lands along the Atlantic Ocean in eastern Canada that Vikings discovered and named Vineland.

The arts flourished in some places. In India, temples were built with hundreds of statues. Indian and Arab craftsmen carved chess pieces that looked like camels and elephants. Lady Murasaki, a Japanese noblewoman, wrote what's considered the world's first novel, "The Tale of Genji," the story of a prince and his many girlfriends.

TOUGH TIMES IN EUROPE

However, life was very difficult in Europe, where most families were poor in the year 1000 AD. Europeans were about the only people in the world who called it 1000, because the calendar we use today had been developed by Christians in Europe to count the years after Jesus' birth. Around the rest of the globe, most people had no idea that Christians thought this was a special year. Native Americans, Chinese, Muslims and Jews were among the many groups of people who had their own calendars with different systems for counting the years.

Today, historians believe that the Christian calendar was wrong about the date of Jesus' birth, because he probably was born around 3 or 4 BC. However, in 1000, Christians believed that their calendar was correct and that exactly one millennium had passed since Jesus' birth. Some people were afraid that the world might end soon

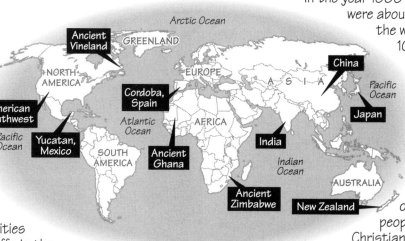

Map labels: Arctic Ocean, Ancient Vineland, GREENLAND, China, NORTH AMERICA, EUROPE, A S I A, Pacific Ocean, Cordoba, Spain, Japan, American Southwest, Atlantic Ocean, AFRICA, Pacific Ocean, Yucatan, Mexico, India, SOUTH AMERICA, Ancient Ghana, Indian Ocean, AUSTRALIA, Ancient Zimbabwe, New Zealand

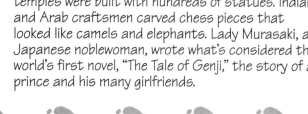

and Jesus would return to send people to heaven and hell.

"The fear spread from family to family by word of mouth — a fear that the world might go up in flames," says Richard Erdoes, a historian. "I think people were pretty scared about what might happen to them."

Other historians disagree with Erdoes and say that the majority of Europeans were so poor and uneducated that most of them may not have been aware of the year at all. Historians do agree, though, that European farms and villages were pretty miserable places in the year 1000.

In 1000, most families farmed and most children helped their parents take care of animals, plow fields, plant and harvest crops. In many places, families also had to spend part of their time working for the local nobleman, perhaps taking care of his home or serving the food in his banquet hall.

Ordinary homes were small and dirty, partly because farm animals often were stabled inside the house right along with the family.

In a few parts of the world, however, people were able to build remarkably well-organized cities.

CITIES OF THE WORLD

In the American Southwest, the Anasazi balanced high-rise cities along rocky cliffs, which protected them if enemies ever tried to attack. These were comfortable dwellings with many rooms.

In west Africa, the kingdom of Ghana became powerful around the year 1000 because it was perfectly situated between the Sahara Desert and the lush woodlands to the south of it. Traders

traveled hundreds of miles from all directions to reach Ghana, where they could trade gold, copper, food and salt.

In southeastern Africa, the rulers of the kingdom of Great Zimbabwe were getting rich from their own gold and copper mines and were building a series of circle-shaped stone fortresses. In 1000, they started building on the top of a high, rocky mountain. Soon, however, they used up all that space. Over the next few centuries, their palaces spilled out across many nearby hillsides. One of these buildings was larger than a football field.

Most people in Ghana and Great Zimbabwe were not that rich, but they probably had healthier and happier lives than Europeans at that time. In the African kingdoms, people had plenty of meat, fruit and vegetables to eat. They had good tools made of wood and metal.

CHECK OUT THE CHORES

✪ Being a kid at the last millennium — or even in the last century — wasn't easy. Go back in time and you'll find that kids had lots of work to do. Thank goodness kids today have dishwashers, vacuum cleaners and lots of modern tools to make chores like cleaning your room faster and easier. Imagine what kids will be doing in the next millennium. Will they have a robot to pick up the toys? Make up a chore list for the kid of the future. If you want, make a drawing of your chore robot and describe what it does.

THE TRAVELERS

Around the Pacific Ocean, people were moving great distances. The Polynesian people in the South Pacific were spreading from island to island and finally reached New Zealand in 1000. In modern times, these first people to settle in New Zealand are called the Maoris.

The Maoris were skilled hunters and fishers. They had beautiful jewelry, tools and weapons, often carved from whale bones and whale teeth.

For many people in Africa and the Pacific rim, the world seemed like a big, exciting place, which is much different than the way most European families looked at the world. In Europe, the world seemed like a pretty small and scary place, often no bigger than the tiny village where a person lived and died.

Nearly 300 years would pass before Marco Polo traveled with his father and his uncle to the court of the emperor Kublai Khan in China, then returned to tell other Europeans about the wonders of the Far East.

PROSPERITY IN THE EAST

In the Far East, emperors ruled China and Japan. Both countries were enjoying a time of peace and prosperity. Wealthy families enjoyed fine foods, poetry and music, and wore expensive, colorful silk clothing.

In China, this period was called the Song Dynasty. For many centuries, the Chinese had sent traders as far as the Middle East to sell their silk cloth. By 1000, the network of caravan routes these traders followed across Asia was known as the Silk Road. However, around this time, these caravans gradually were being replaced by ships that reached the same destination by sea.

In Japan, the Fujiwara family had dominated the government for a long time. Lady Murasaki was part of that family and lived in the imperial court. She thought it was funny that the rich people around her devoted so much attention to frivolous things, such as the latest fashions or competitions that were held to paint the most beautiful pictures.

She wrote diaries and then her long novel about life in the imperial court. Many historians consider "The Tale of Genji" to be the world's first novel — or, at least, the oldest surviving novel.

VIKING EXPLORATION

The Vikings were one group of Europeans who were known for traveling great distances in 1000, although their reputation was terrifying. Their voyages usually ended in murderous attacks on defenseless villages.

The first European to visit Greenland, Eric the Red, went to sea because he had killed two men in Iceland. His son, Leif, was inspired by Eric's adventures and sailed all the way to what is now eastern Canada in 1000. He called the place Vineland because of the wild grapes he found growing there. Soon, Leif's stories about the natural riches in this new land reached Europe and many other Vikings followed him.

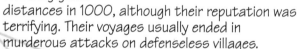

THE BEST PLACE IN 1000?

There was at least one city in Europe whose health, wealth and culture ranked among the best places on earth: Cordoba, a Muslim city in what is now Spain that was one of the world's leading centers of learning in 1000.

Unlike Christians at that time, Muslims were encouraged to study science. In 1000, for example, the Muslim scientist Alhazen was studying everything from the way human eyes work to the way planets move through the universe.

"The biggest library in central Europe had 5,000 books, but the library in Cordoba had more than 300,000," says Erdoes. "In Cordoba, skilled Jewish and Muslim doctors took care of people. There was a sewer system to keep the streets clean. There were 100 public baths.

"Life was hard for most people," says Erdoes. "But, if you had to live anywhere in 1000 AD, Cordoba was the best place to live."

By David Crumm

BACK TO THE FUTURE

✪ We've taken you back 1,000 years; now let's leap ahead. Put yourself in the year 3000. Pretend you're a newspaper editor. What will be today's headlines in news, sports, fashion and entertainment? What discoveries will be reported? What will be for sale in the advertisements? Does it even look like the newspaper of today? Is your newspaper on-line — or do people get news in some way we haven't thought of yet?

FUTURE FUN AND GAMES

When your parents were kids, they watched cartoon shows like the "Jetsons" and "Scooby-Doo." The cartoons are still here — but now there are 24-hour cartoon channels. The toys they played with are still here, too — like Barbies, yo-yos and Monopoly. But your toybox has gone high-tech.

For entertainment, they played pinball at the roller rink — and later on, there was Pong and the first generation of video games. Now you can play Pong on your CD-ROM.

And speaking of video games, wow! Your parents couldn't even dream up the stuff you play today. The gaming systems,

Disney Quest is leading the way for play places of the future.

including Nintendo 64 and Sony's Playstation, are creative, smart and fun. And they're getting better fast. Sega's new Dreamcast is setting a new standard for high-tech graphics. Expect computer gaming to become faster, smarter, cheaper and even more amazing in the coming years.

Now come along with the Yak to explore some of the ways you'll have fun in the future.

PLAY PLACES

Where will families go for fun in the new millennium? To find out, the Yak headed for ... Chicago. Yup, Chicago. Why? Well, the city has gone millennium crazy, with a new park for kids and loads of millennium activities. They've even created a millennium dance (if you visit, watch for dance steps spray-painted on the sidewalks).

But that's not why the Yak visited. The Yak wanted to check out the latest entertainment concepts: Disney Quest and ESPN zone. So far, Chicago is

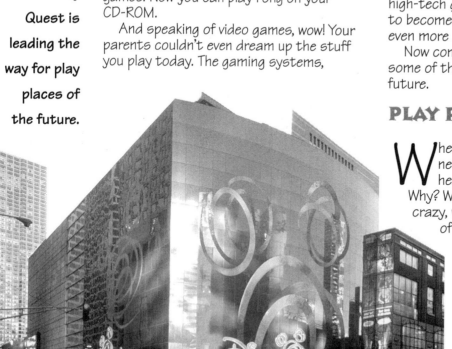

the only city with both these play places.

Both places represent the future of family play. Think of them as high-tech entertainment centers where families can play, eat and shop under one BIG roof.

Disney Quest is really an interactive fun house — and an example of things to come. It's five stories of virtual reality games and video games.

ESPN Zone has walls of TV sets tuned to ESPN, of course, plus every interactive sports game you can imagine.

It's the job of Arthur Levitt III, president of Disney Regional Entertainment, to develop new ideas and help plan the sites.

But don't look for a Disney Quest to open in your backyard in time for millennium celebrations. By 2001, there will be three Disney Quest locations: Orlando, Chicago and Philadelphia, where one is being developed.

ESPN Zone is also open in Baltimore and New York, with new ones opening in Atlanta and Washington, D.C., in 2000.

"I think technology will play a more and more significant role in out-of-home

entertainment for families," says Levitt.

As technology becomes more available and user-friendly, we'll see lots of changes in the way we play, adds Levitt. Not every place will have the magic — or money — of Disney, but even local arcades will have upgraded games and virtual reality experiences in the near future.

And people will have all kinds of cool virtual reality experiences at home, too. Of course, the games won't be as fancy as the ones at Disney Quest or other entertainment centers — that would be too expensive — but you, and someday, your kids, will have amazing virtual reality games and toys at home.

POKEMON AND BEYOND

What else will you play in the next millennium? "Right now, Pokemon rules!" says toy expert Chris Byrne, who has been writing about the toy industry for 20 years.

And Byrne thinks you'll want to catch 'em all for at least another year or two. Maybe longer.

Chris says kids are in the driver's seat when it comes to toys. You have the power to create the next craze. Kids' buying power shapes the kinds of toys that are created and sold. Need proof? Just look at all the Pokemon stuff beyond Nintendo Game

Boy games and Wizards of the Coast Pokemon cards. Pokemon has created a line of spinoff toys, T-shirts, stickers, school supplies, posters, board games ...

But things change fast in the world of toys.

Remember virtual pets, another toy trend from Japan? And how about Beanie Babies — after several hot years, the critters are tired and retired.

Even if virtual pets and Beanies are so yesterday, both trends tell us something about what will be hot tomorrow.

Companies like Ty, the maker of Beanies, probably will be back with something new to collect in the 21st Century. Pokemon is proof you still love to collect toys.

Virtual pets and Furbys were big fads for a while. You may not be playing with them now, but don't toss your critters. In the new millennium, your '90s toys may become collectibles. But, because technology is changing so fast, toys like Furby won't seem so amazing in the future.

What is amazing now? Amazing Ally, a high-tech doll from Playmates. She's really a computer in a dress, Byrne jokes. As technology becomes more available, dolls like Ally will be the norm. They will do more and cost less.

OLD FAVORITES

But you'll still play with low-tech toys in the future. Board games and yo-yos were popular with your parents and they'll be popular with your children someday. The wildly popular "Harry Potter" books by J.K. Rowling are a great example of how something low-tech can bewitch millions of kids, says Byrne. The "Harry Potter" books, about an orphan boy and his adventures at Hogwarts School of Witchcraft and Wizardry, are creative and magical. Toys don't have to walk, talk or beep to be cool.

Generation Girls are modern Barbies.

FROM GREEN SLIME TO PRIME TIME

Sometimes you don't want to do anything at all — you just want to be entertained. That's where Nickelodeon comes in. It's hard to imagine, but when your parents were young there were only a handful of TV channels. Cable TV was new, and no one was creating TV networks just for kids. Not until Nickelodeon, anyway.

In 1999, Nickelodeon, the granddaddy of kids' TV, celebrated its 20th birthday. The folks at Nick like to say they've gone "from green slime to prime time." And they have, creating some of the most popular TV characters ever and setting the standard for kids' TV. You can thank Nick for the Disney Channel, Cartoon Network and all the newer networks that are aimed at you.

What will the top kids' network be up to in the 21st Century?

In terms of the way you watch TV, nothing dramatic will be happening in the next three or four years, says Cyma Zarghami, executive vice president and general manager of Nickelodeon.

But TV will probably be interactive in the future. "One of the things that will become more natural is the idea of multi-tasking — you'll be on-line while you're watching TV while you're talking on the phone," says Zarghami. "There will be one box where it all happens."

Nick is already working to join TV with the Internet through interactive sites that connect Web activities to what you're watching on TV.

Expect more interactive TV — and more live experiences with TV like concert tours and theme park tie-ins.

The Yak visited Nickelodeon Studios.

All the success of Nickelodeon has caught the attention of other television folks. That's good news for kids because it means you have more choices and better shows. TV is following YOUR script.

By Janis Campbell

MAKE A TIME CAPSULE

Pack a present for the future. Imagine, 50 years from now, opening up a time capsule.

If your mom and dad had made a time capsule when they were kids, they might have included an ID bracelet, a vinyl lunchbox, a music record and maybe a box from a TV dinner.

Boy, things have changed.

Now you have friendship or hemp bracelets and thermal lunch bags. And your capsule would have a CD and a microwave dinner box — both things your mom and dad didn't grow up with.

That's exactly what makes time capsules so much fun. Imagine someday opening yours up and sharing it with your own kids. The millennium makes it all the more historic.

You can make your own capsule.

HERE'S WHAT TO DO:

First, gather the items to put in the capsule. Collect things that reflect your personality and the time you're living in. Here's a list of some ideas to get you started:

✪ Your favorite CD. (You can just put in the box and liner notes.)

✪ The packaging from your favorite snack or meal. (Make sure it's clean — you don't want mold growing in your millennium capsule.)

✪ A favorite fashion (something you've outgrown, of course).

✪ School papers — maybe your writing

Photo by J. Kyle Keener

journal, a reading worksheet, spelling test or any sample of your best work.
❂ Pictures of you, your family and your best friends.
❂ Ribbons or trophies.
❂ A magazine, newspaper or TV guide.
❂ Fad toys or trinkets (like a yo-yo, Beanie Baby or butterfly hair clips).
❂ Collectible cards (a baseball or Pokemon card).
❂ A favorite book (or you could put in the book cover if it's a hardback).
❂ Sports souvenirs (ticket stubs from a big game or a pennant from your favorite team).
❂ A school concert program.
❂ A birthday party invitation.
❂ Anything you think reflects you at the start of the millennium.

Next, find a container to use as your capsule. You can use an airtight plastic storage container. The size is up to you. The bigger it is, the more you can store.

Finally, your capsule is ready to pack. Now you need to find a safe, dry place to store it. Talk to your parents about the best place to store your capsule. It can be as simple a place as the back of a linen closet or a pantry shelf. Even under your bed is fine. The Yak thinks it's fine to put it in a place where you can look at it from time to time.

By Cathy Collison and Janis Campbell

Photo courtesy of Old Navy

You may not want to put your favorite vest in a capsule, but you could put in a tag or a photo of you modeling it.

EXTRA CREDIT

If you want, make a second capsule as a group effort at school. Your class — or your entire school — can make a capsule to store in the school.

Here's how to start:
❂ Talk to your teacher and principal about making the capsule as a class or school project.
❂ Ask everyone to write a prediction about the future and place it in the capsule.
❂ Take a school survey on what items to include in the capsule to represent your school. For example, you can include a yearbook, a school T-shirt, a symbol of your school (do you have a mascot?), the school lunch menu, a concert or play program, school handbook or rules and school newsletter. You could also include a social studies book, student essays and artwork.

TIME TO PARTY

People around the world are celebrating the millennium. Here are some ideas to help carry out your millennium theme.

GETTING READY

Make your own invitations using paper plates. Turn a paper plate into a clock face by decorating with numbers and hands. On it, write your party invitation: time, place and date. For party favors, send your guests home with more timely trinkets like mini-timers, plastic watches and fortune cookies.

Photo by J. Kyle Keener

ENTERTAINMENT

Here are some movies to get you in the millennium mood. You can watch them anytime this year, but they'd be a great way to pass the time at your parties. These are fantasies and science fiction — some go into the future and some into the past. Enjoy!

"Blast from the Past"
"Star Wars" and "Star Trek" movies
"Planet of the Apes"
"The Time Machine"
"Fahrenheit 451"
Episodes from "The Jetsons"
"Flubber"
"2001: A Space Odyssey"
"Back to the Future," I, II and III

NOISEMAKING

Set your clocks so all the alarms, timers and buzzers in your house go off at midnight!

GAMES

Do some fortune-telling: Recruit your mom or grandma to be Madame Future! Do a half-hour of fortune-telling. She can use your Magic Eight-Ball.

What to serve at midnight? Here's an idea that takes the cake. Make or buy a round cake. Decorate it with hands and numbers.

PERSONALITY PREDICTIONS

Ask your party guests to predict which party-goer will have which famous job. Take a vote at your party. Here are some suggested categories. Tally the votes and then announce the predictions before midnight.

- ❑ Future president of the U.S.
- ❑ Future business tycoon
- ❑ Future movie star
- ❑ Future sports star
- ❑ First person on Mars
- ❑ Future inventor

Ticktock, it's time to rock! Try the Yak's party tips for your own millennium celebration.

A TIME TO REMEMBER

Get an instant or disposable camera and snap some memorable pictures. Make copies for all your friends who were at the party.

FUTURE SEERS

Make a list of leaders in science, politics and exploration who changed history — leaders who were ahead of their time. Play a charades-style game. You can make speeches or act out. But you can't say the name of the person you represent or what he or she did. Write each name on a separate slip of paper and let guests draw a name. You can play alone or in teams. (Here's a fun one to start with: Alexander Graham Bell, who is credited with inventing the telephone.)

By Cathy Collison and Janis Campbell

Photo by J. Kyle Keener

2001 BUBBLES

Your kitchen is packed with celebration supplies. Lots of people bang pots and pans with spoons to ring in the year. But you have other goodies at hand for celebration. Whip up a batch of bubbles using dish detergent, sugar and water (try using 1/4 cup detergent, 1 cup water and 1 tablespoon of sugar). For bubble wands, use slotted spatulas or your favorite wands. The more the merrier!

MAKE A MILLENNIUM JOURNAL

The passing of the millennium is something to mark. You'll want to remember this historic time in big ways and small. The best way to remember is to write it all down. Mark the milestones with your millennium journal.

I am _____ years old.   I am _____ inches tall.

I weigh _____ pounds.

MY
SCHOOL
PICTURE

THESE ARE MY BEST FRIENDS.

MY FAVORITE THINGS ARE

_____

_____

_____

_____

_____

_____

_____

HERE ARE
MY PETS
(or stuffed animals).

**THE COOLEST THING
THAT HAPPENED TO
ME THIS YEAR WAS**

_____

_____

_____

_____

_____

_____

_____

ME ON A
SPECIAL DAY.

HERE I AM!

JOURNAL

MY FAMILY

OUR MILLENNIUM PICTURE.

WE TOOK A VACATION TO

_____

_____

_____

_____

_____

I INTERVIEWED MY FAMILY ABOUT THE MILLENNIUM. HERE ARE THEIR PREDICTIONS ABOUT THE FUTURE:

MOM:

_____

_____

_____

_____

_____

_____

_____

DAD:

_____

_____

_____

_____

_____

_____

_____

GRANDPARENTS:

_____

_____

_____

_____

_____

_____

_____

_____

MY HOUSE

HERE'S WHERE WE LIVE.

J O U R N A L

FUN AND GAMES

MY FRIENDS AND I PLAY: _____

_____

_____

_____

I COLLECT: _____

_____

_____

_____

MY FAVORITE BOOKS: _____

_____

_____

_____

MY FAVORITE TV SHOWS: _____

_____

_____

_____

MY FAVORITE MOVIES: _____

_____

_____

_____

MY FAVORITE MUSIC: _____

_____

_____

_____

THE HOTTEST FASHION TREND: _____

_____

_____

_____

MY FAVORITE FOODS: _____

_____

_____

_____

THE HOTTEST DANCE CRAZE: _____

_____

_____

_____

MY FAVORITE VIDEO GAMES: _____

_____

_____

_____

SCHOOL STUFF

MY FAVORITE TEACHERS: _____

_____

_____

_____

MY FAVORITE FIELD TRIP: _____

_____

_____

_____

THE STRANGEST SCHOOL RULE IS:

_____

_____

MY FAVORITE SUBJECTS: _____

_____

_____

_____

MY FAVORITE HOT LUNCH IS: _____

_____

_____

COST OF SCHOOL LUNCH: _____

_____

WHAT I DID AT RECESS: _____

_____

_____

_____

**THE BIGGEST NEWS
AT SCHOOL THIS YEAR WAS:**

_____

_____

_____

_____

THE BEST SCHOOL PARTY WAS:

_____

_____

_____

IN THE NEWS

THE BIGGEST NEWS STORIES:

_____

_____

_____

_____

THE TOP SPORTS STORIES:

_____

_____

_____

_____

Photos by J. Kyle Keener

MY TOWN WAS IN THE NEWS BECAUSE

_____

_____

_____

_____

THE BIGGEST WEATHER STORY:

_____

_____

_____

_____

SPORTS

MY FAVORITE TEAMS:

_____

_____

_____

RECORD-BREAKERS

Name	Sport
_____	_____
_____	_____
_____	_____

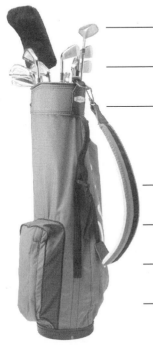

MY FAVORITE SPORTS STARS:

_____

_____

_____

_____

J O U R N A L

SPORTS

THESE ARE THE SPORTS I PLAYED:

_____   _____

_____   _____

_____   _____

_____   _____

ME AND MY TEAM.

HERE I AM CELEBRATING.

HERE'S WHAT I WILL REMEMBER MOST
ABOUT THE PASSING OF THE MILLENNIUM: —————————

_____

_____

_____

_____

_____

_____

YAKLENNIUM

J O U R N A L

MY FAVORITE
MILLENNIUM PHOTO.

MY MILLENNIUM WISH LIST:

These are my hopes and my wishes
for the next couple of years:

And, for the next 1,000 years:

_____

_____

_____

_____

_____

_____

_____

Journal by Janis Campbell and Cathy Collison